Commissioned by His Eminence, Cardinal Heenan, Archbishop _____ *dedicated*
to Colin Mawby and the Choir of Westminste _____

MASS FOR FIVE V

KYRIE

GLORIA

Meno vivo ♩ = 100

...Soon the music has to go out of print.

SANCTUS

Più mosso

BENEDICTUS

AGNUS DEI

28

The Chester Books of Motets

The first sixteen volumes of this expanding series are devoted to wide range of sacred renaissance motets with Latin texts, and contain a mixture of well known and unfamiliar pieces, some of which are published here for the first time. All appear in completely new editions by Anthony G. Petti.

1. The Italian School for 4 voices
2. The English School for 4 voices
3. The Spanish School for 4 voices
4. The German School for 4 voices
5. The Flemish School for 4 voices
6. Christmas and Advent Motets for 4 voices
7. Motets for 3 voices
8. The French School for 4 voices
9. The English School for 5 voices
10. The Italian and Spanish Schools for 5 voices
11. The Flemish and German Schools for 5 voices
12. Christmas and Advent Motets for 5 voices
13. The English School for 6 voices
14. The Italian and Spanish Schools for 6 voices
15. The Flemish and German Schools for 6 voices
16. Christmas and Advent Motets for 6 voices

An index, complete with suggested seasonal use, covering the first sixteen books of the series, is printed in Book 16.

CHESTER MUSIC
(Part of the Music Sales Group)
14 -15 Berners street, London W1T 3LJ, UK

Choral Works by
Lennox Berkeley

Secular Choral Works

Ask me no more/TTBB
Signs in the Dark/SATB and String Orchestra
Spring at this hour/SSATBB
The Hill of the Graces/SSAATTBB
Three Songs for Male Voices/TTBB

Sacred Choral Works with English Text

A Festival Anthem/SATB and Organ
Batter my heart, three person'd God/
Soprano, Chorus and Chamber Orchestra
Look up sweet babe/Soprano and SATB
Lord when the sense of Thy sweet grace/SATB and Organ
Missa Brevis/SATB and Organ
Sweet was the song/SATB and Organ
The Lord is my Shepherd/Treble Solo, SATB and Organ
Thou hast made me/SATB and Organ

Sacred Choral Works with Latin Text

Domini est terra/SATB and Orchestra
Magnificat/SATB and Orchestra
Mass for five voices/SSATB
Missa Brevis/SATB and Organ
Salve Regina/Unison
Stabat Mater/SSATBB Soli and 12 Instruments
Also arranged by Michael Berkeley for Soloists and Chamber Orchestra

Three Latin Motets/SSATB
Judica Me/SSATBB

ISBN 0-7119-4781-3

9 780711 947818

ISBN-13: 978-0-7119-4781-8

DISTRIBUTED BY
HAL LEONARD
14004170

8 84088 43981 1

UK.

Order No. CH08845